# Community Helpers

# Bakers

by Tami Deedrick

**Content Consultant:**
Greg Mistell
Executive Director
The Bread Bakers Guild of America

# Bridgestone Books

an imprint of Capstone Press

Bridgestone Books are published by Capstone Press
818 North Willow Street, Mankato, Minnesota 56001
http://www.capstone-press.com

*Library of Congress Cataloging-in-Publication Data*
Deedrick, Tami.
    Bakers/by Tami Deedrick.
        p. cm.--(Community helpers)
    Includes bibliographical references and index.
    Summary:  Briefly describes the tasks, clothing, and education of a baker. Includes a
recipe for peanut butter cookies.
    ISBN 1-56065-728-6
    1. Bakers and bakeries--Juvenile literature.  2. Baking--Juvenile literature.  [1. Bakers and
bakeries.  2. Baking.  3. Occupations.]  I. Title.  II. Series: Community helpers  (Mankato, Minn.)
TX763.D37  1998
641.8'15--dc21

                                    97-38174
                                       CIP
                                        AC

**Editorial credits**
Editor, Matt Doeden; cover design, Timothy Halldin; photo research, Michelle L. Norstad
**Photo credits**
International Stock/Greg Edwards, cover; George Ancona, 12
Unicorn Stock/Jean Higgins, 4, 6; Robert Vankirk, 8; Jeff Greenburg, 10, 14, 16;
   Joseph Sohm, 18; Tom McCarthy, 20

# Table of Contents

## Bakers

A baker's job is to bake. Bakers bake bread and rolls. They bake cookies, cakes, and pies. The foods that bakers make are called baked goods.

## Where Bakers Work

Most bakers work in bakeries. A bakery is where people make and sell baked goods. Some bakeries are in grocery stores. A grocery store is a place that sells many kinds of food.

## What Bakers Do

Bakers go to work early. They often start working before the sun rises. Bakers put some baked goods in bags. They mark the bags with prices. Bakers also keep bakeries clean.

## What Bakers Wear

Bakers wear white uniforms. They wear white hats. Some bakers wear aprons. An apron is a cloth that covers a baker's clothes. Bakers usually wear gloves when they make baked goods.

## Tools Bakers Use

Bakers use mixers to make dough. Dough is a sticky mix used in preparing baked goods. Bakers use large pans and ovens when they bake dough. Bakers use hot pads when they reach into ovens. Hot pads keep bakers from burning their hands.

## Bakers and Holidays

Bakers help people enjoy holidays. They bake holiday cakes and cookies. They also bake birthday cakes. Bakers use frosting to draw pictures and write names on cakes.

## Bakers and School

Bakers go to baking school. They learn recipes. A recipe is a set of steps for preparing food. Bakers learn how to make many kinds of baked goods. They practice baking cookies, cakes, breads, and other baked goods.

## People Who Help Bakers

Drivers help bakers by bringing baked goods to people. Farmers supply milk and eggs to make dough. Some bakers have assistants. An assistant helps the baker make baked goods.

## How Bakers Help Others

Bakers make baked goods for the community. A community is a group of people living in one area. Bakers make foods that help people stay healthy. They also make foods that taste good.

# Hands On: Bake Cookies

Bakers make cookies and other foods. Here is an easy recipe for peanut butter cookies. The recipe does not need flour.

## What You Need

1 cup peanut butter          1 bowl
1 cup sugar                       1 or 2 baking pans
1 egg                                 1 fork

## What You Do

1. Ask an adult to help you.
2. Heat the oven to 350 degrees.
3. Put the peanut butter, sugar, and egg in the bowl. Mix them with the fork.
4. Roll the mix into small balls. Make the balls about one inch (2.5 centimeters) wide.
5. Put the balls on the baking pan. Flatten them with the fork. Use a second baking pan if needed.
6. Bake for 10 minutes.
7. Take the pan out of the oven. Let the cookies cool before you eat them.

# Words to Know

**apron** (AY-pruhn)—a cloth that covers a baker's clothes

**baked goods** (BAYKT GUDZ)—the foods that bakers bake

**bakery** (BAYK-ree)—a place where people make and sell baked goods

**community** (kuh-MYOO-nuh-tee)—a group of people living in one area

**dough** (DOH)—a sticky mix used in preparing baked goods.

**grocery store** (GROH-suh-ree STOR)—a place that sells many kinds of food

**recipe** (RESS-i-pee)—a set of steps used to prepare food

# Read More

**Drew, Helen**. *Let's Bake a Cake.* New York: Dorling Kindersley Family Library, 1997.

**Gore, Sheila**. *My Cake.* Milwaukee: Gareth Stevens, 1995.

**Morris, Ann**. *Bread, Bread, Bread.* New York: Mulberry Books, 1993.

# Internet Sites

**Alpha Bakery**
http://www.mysupermarket.com/Greatfood/Kids
**Holsum Intro Page**
http://www.holsum.com
**Kids Cooking Club–Fun Recipes for Children**
http://www.kidscook.com/recipe.htm

# Index